Yummy Treats
An Adult Coloring Book

Calm down and relieve stress by coloring in some delicious treats.

by Victoria Clarke

Illustrated by Ștefania Bălăucă

Stay Calm and Color On!

Hey there!

Coloring has become an inexpensive and fun way to relieve stress and unwind after a busy day doing whatever it is you do!

Whether you work all day or take care of children or simply feel like the world is caving in, take some time to yourself and color in some of these tasty treats.

Including yummy things such as donuts and cupcakes, this coloring book will help you bring your stress levels down without adding in the extra calories of actually eating the food…

Though feel free to eat and color (that's what I do)!

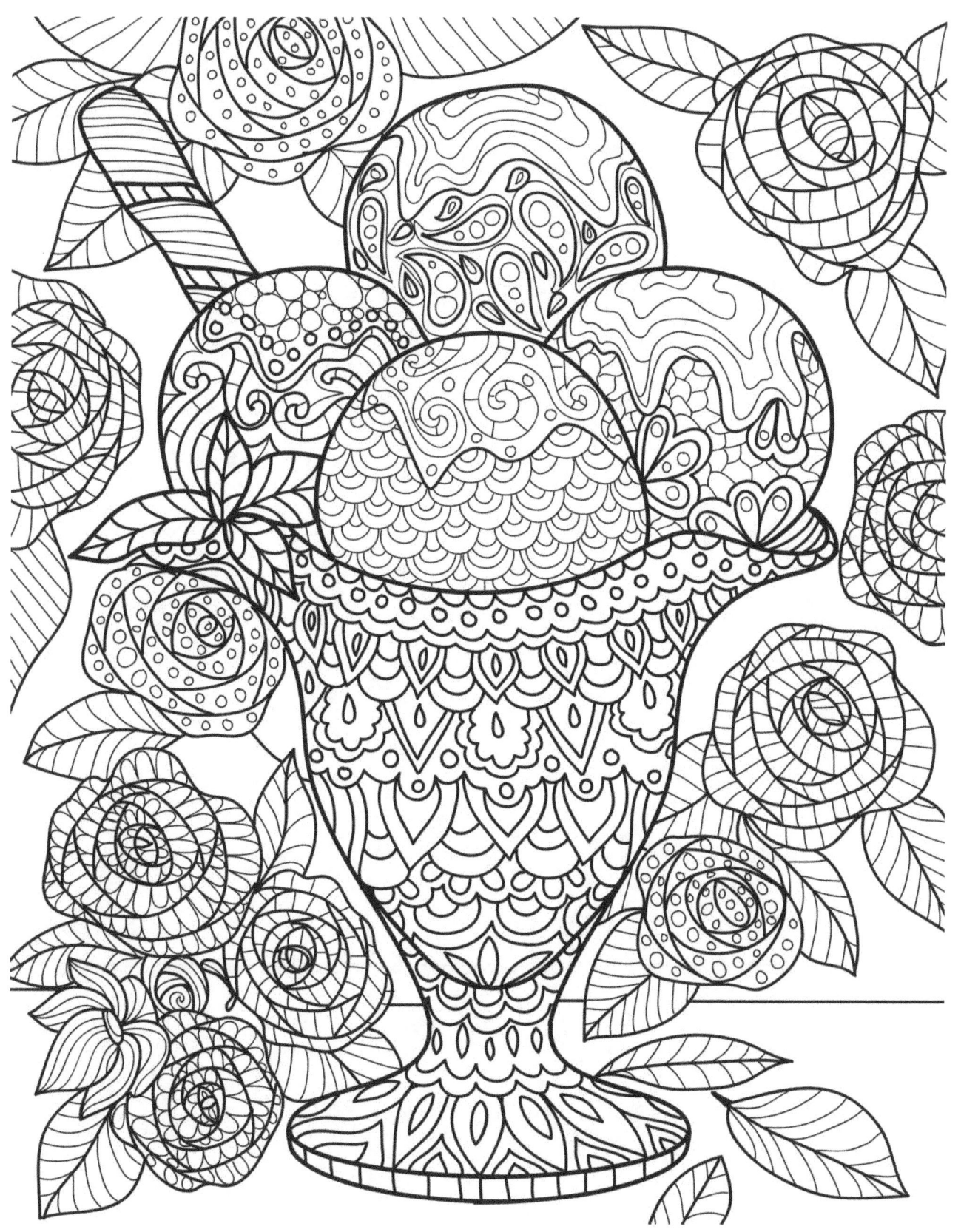

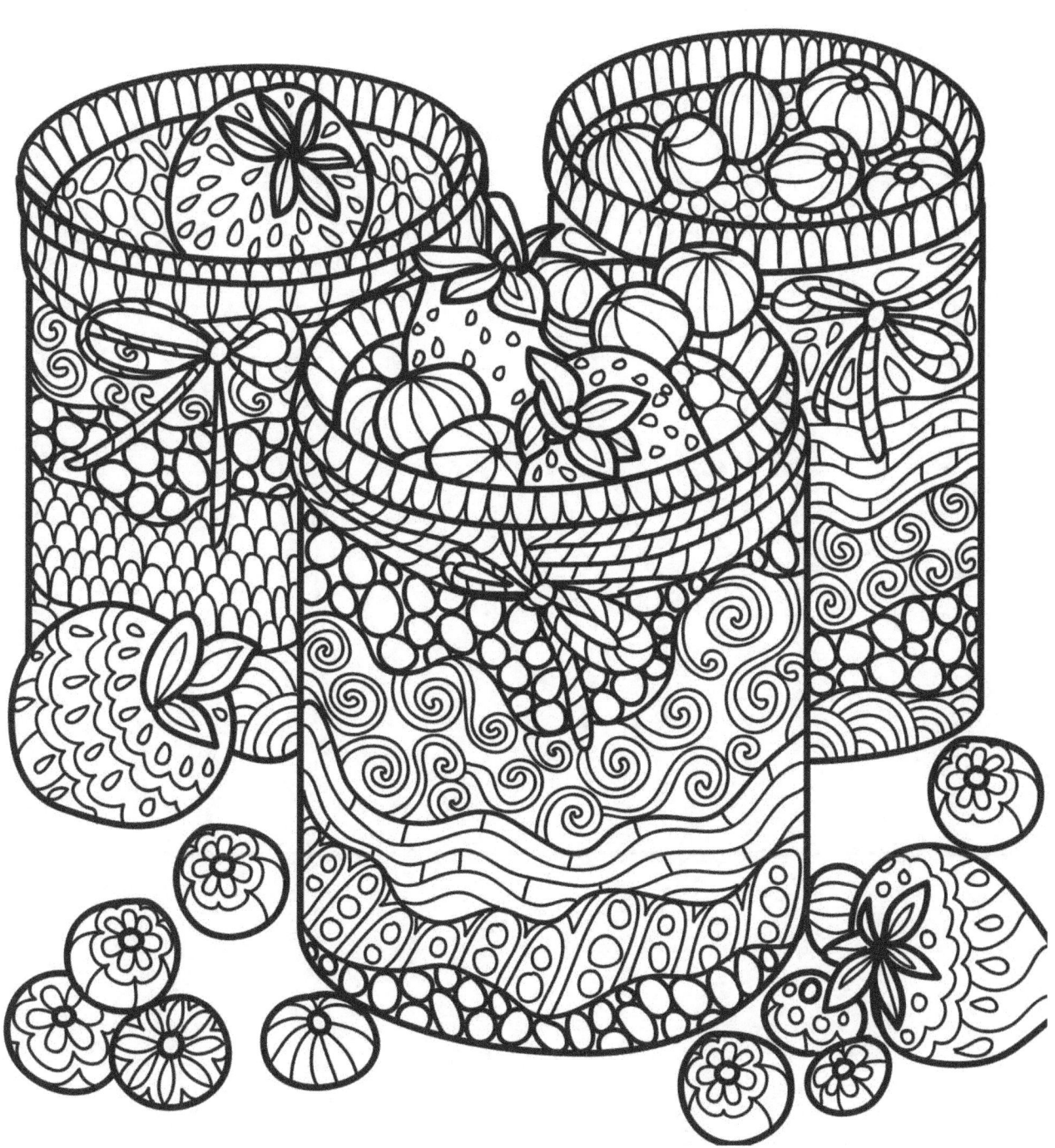

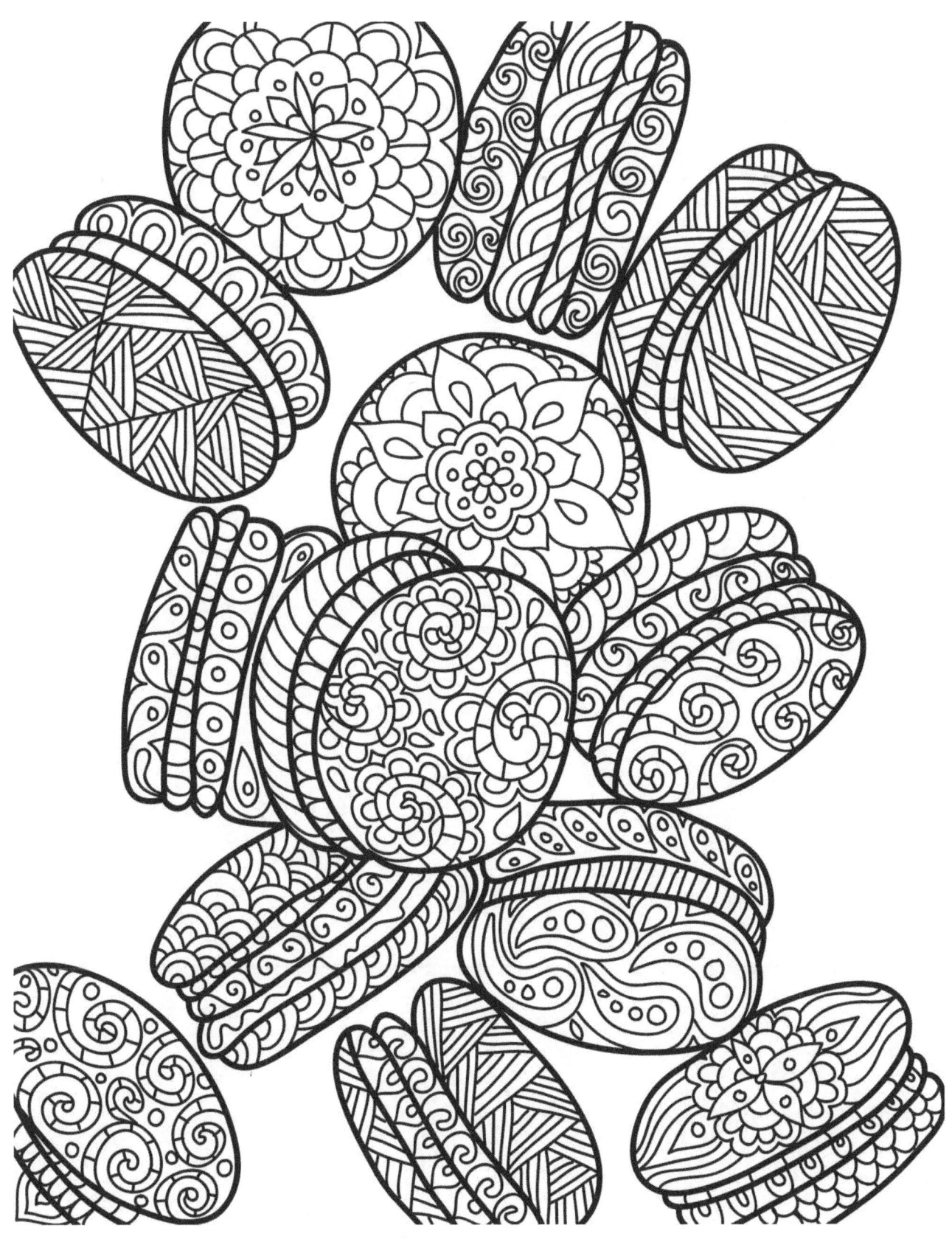

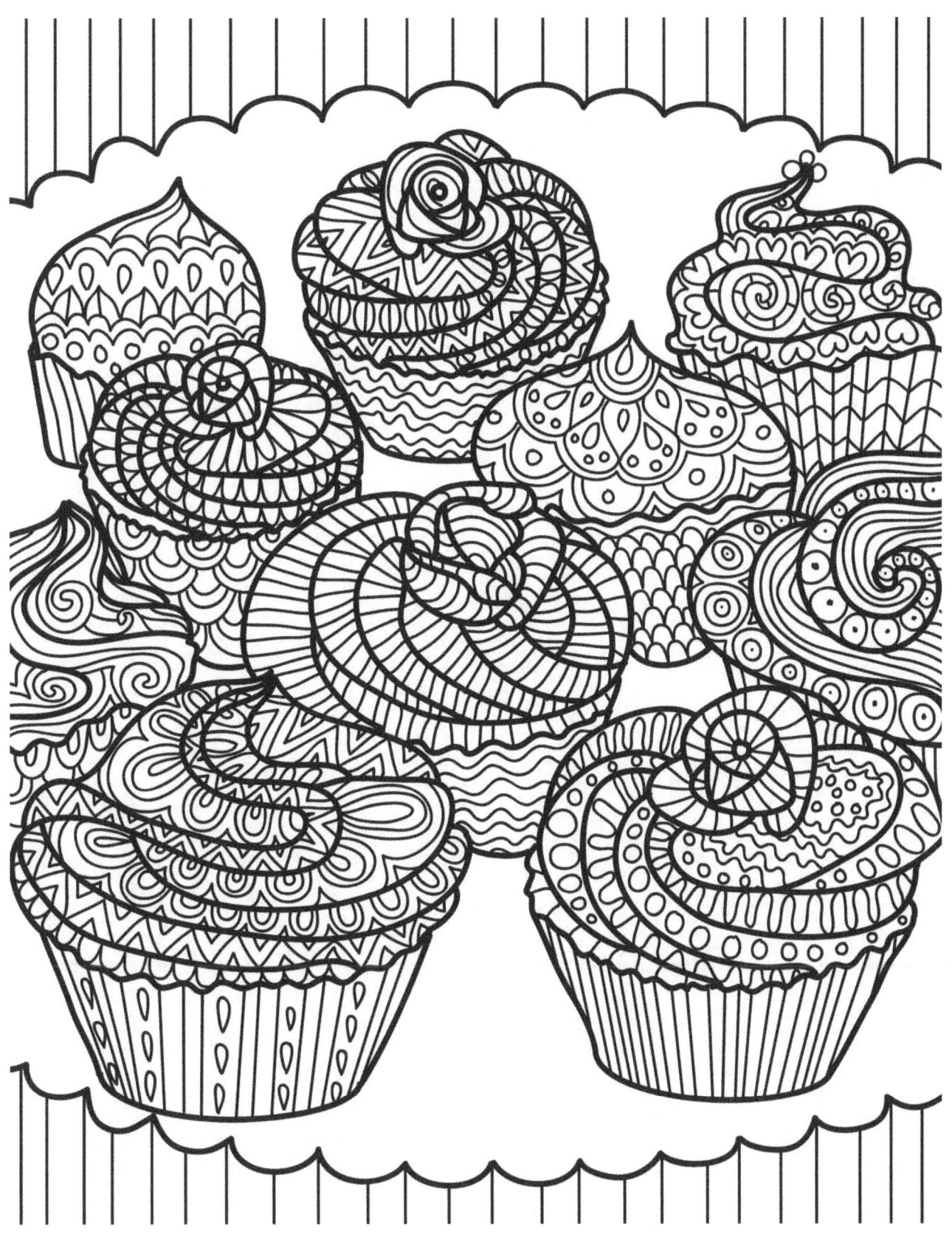

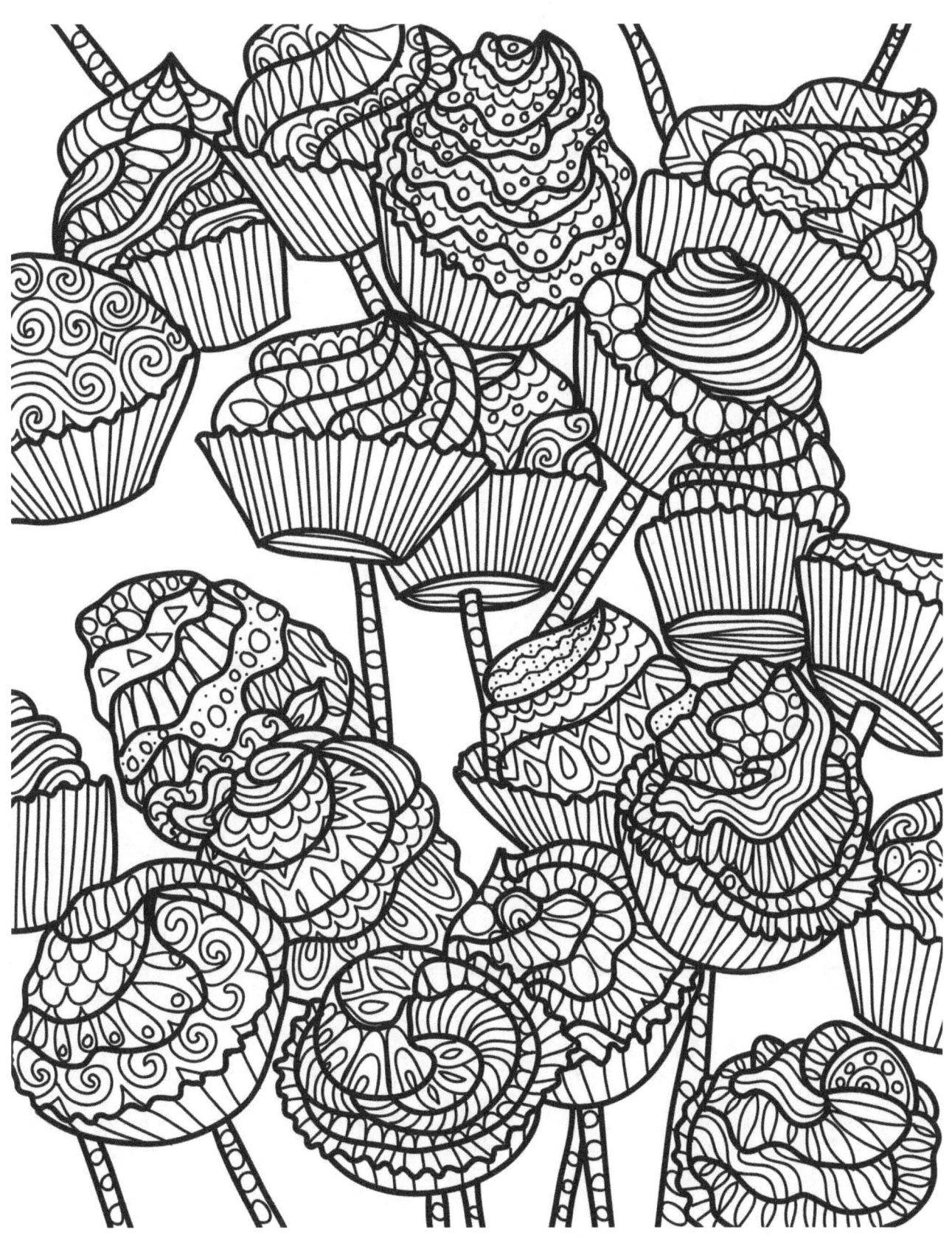

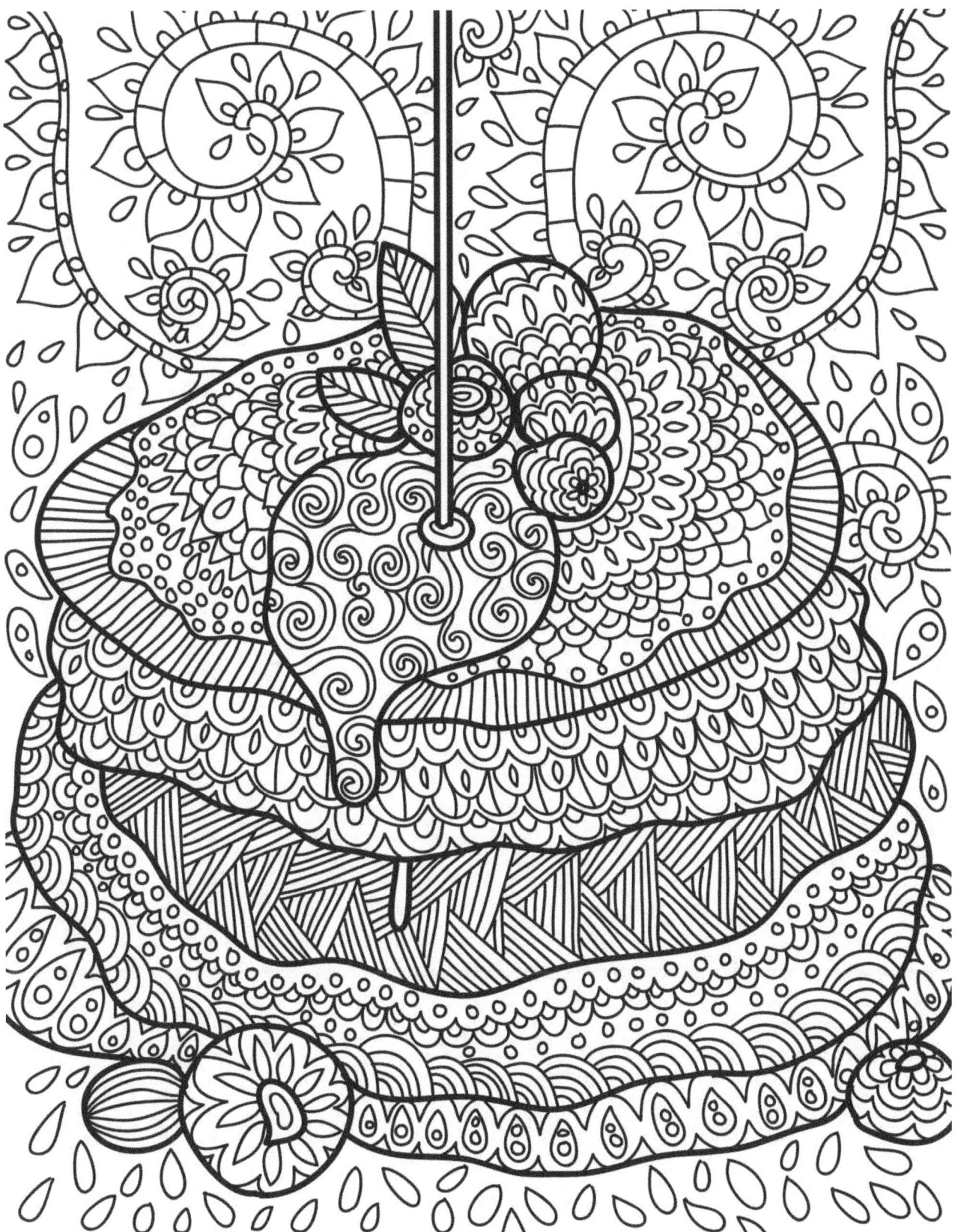

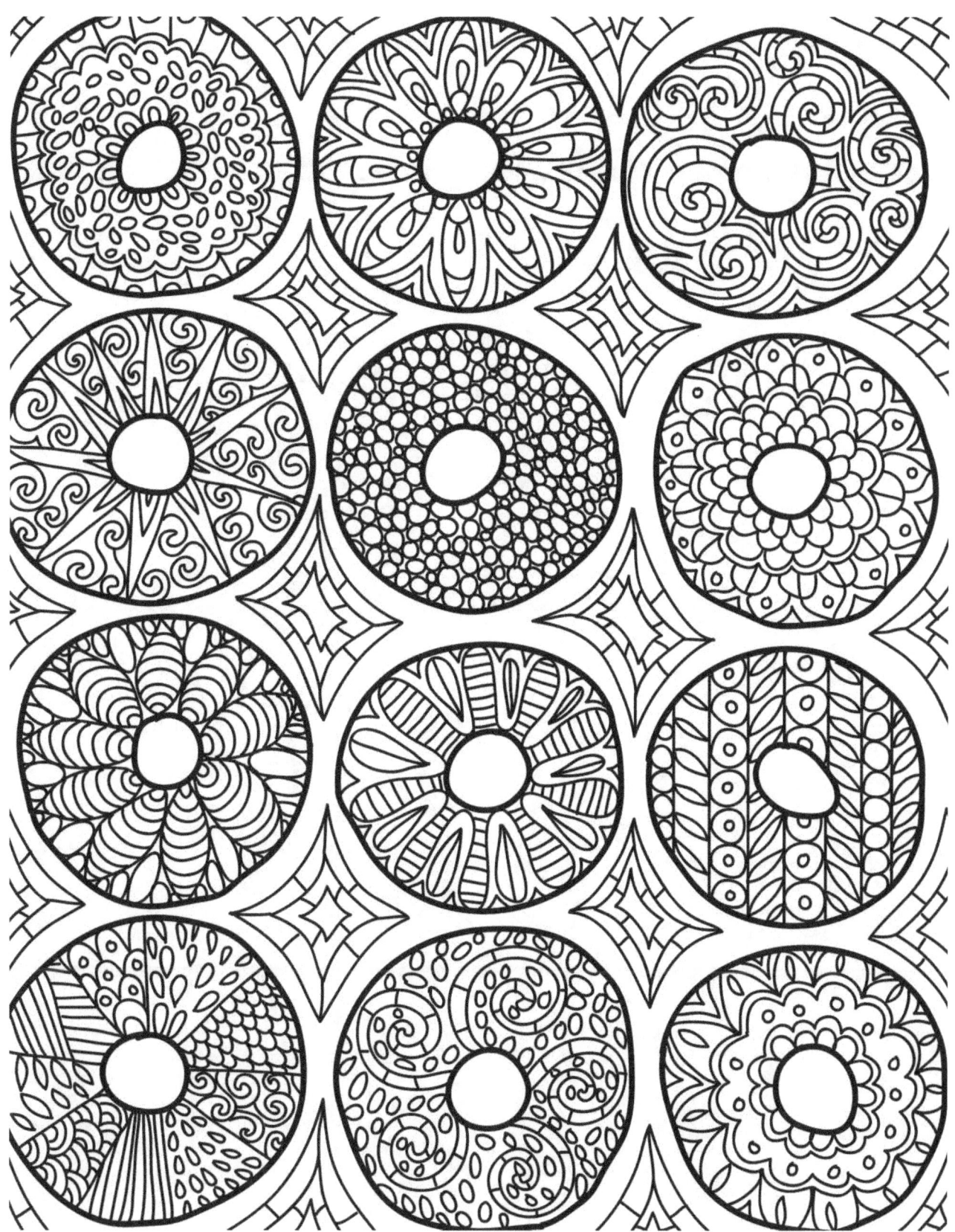

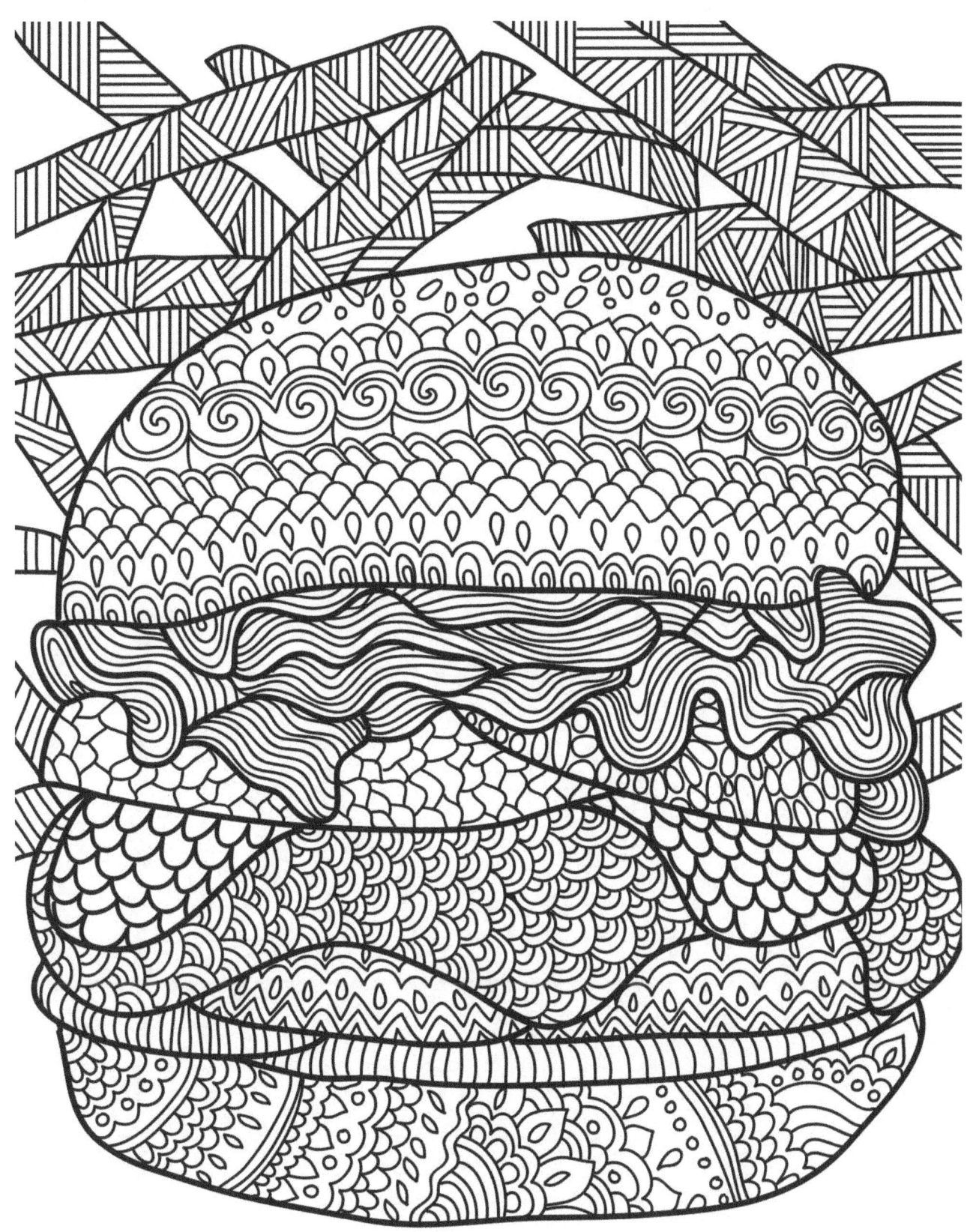

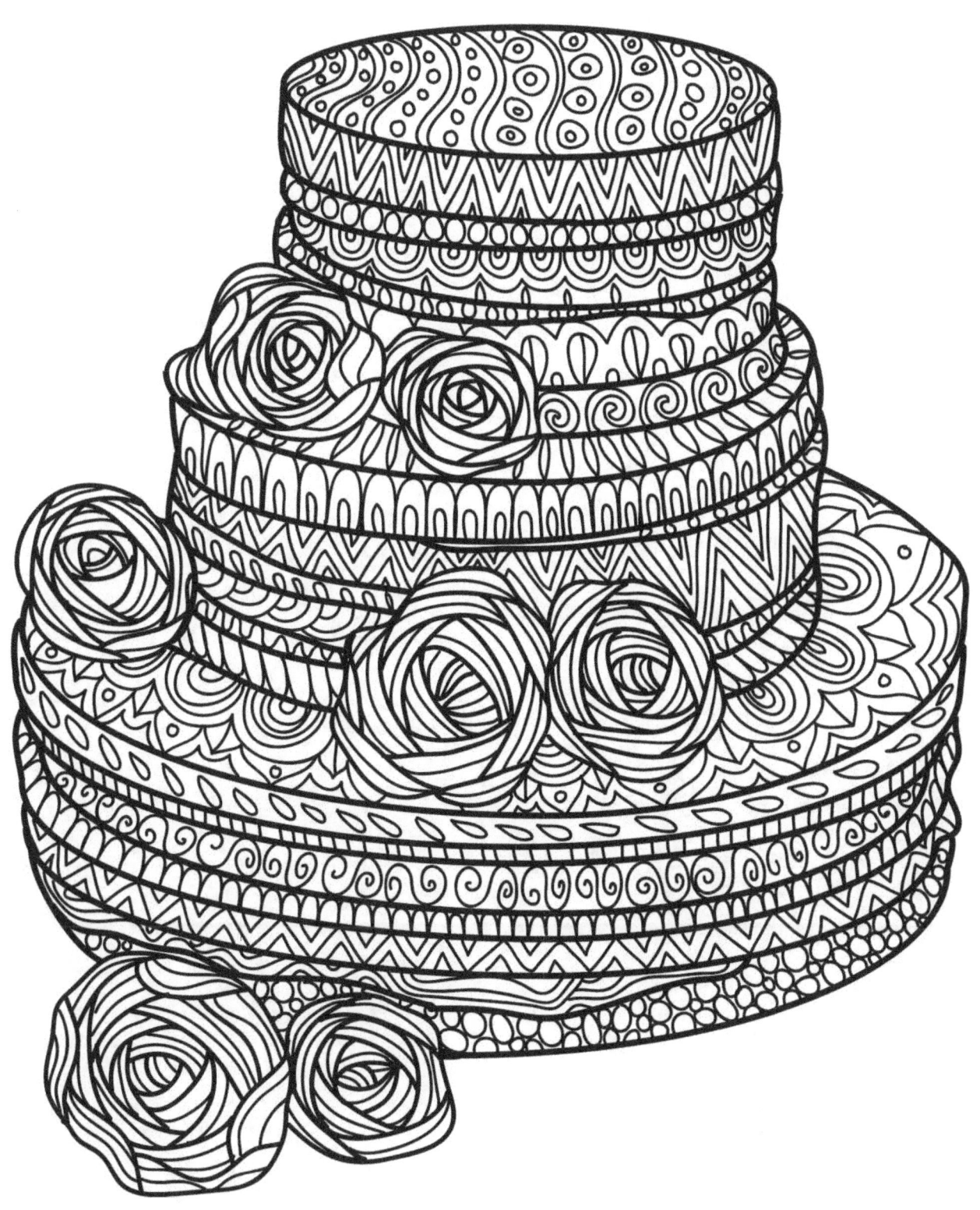

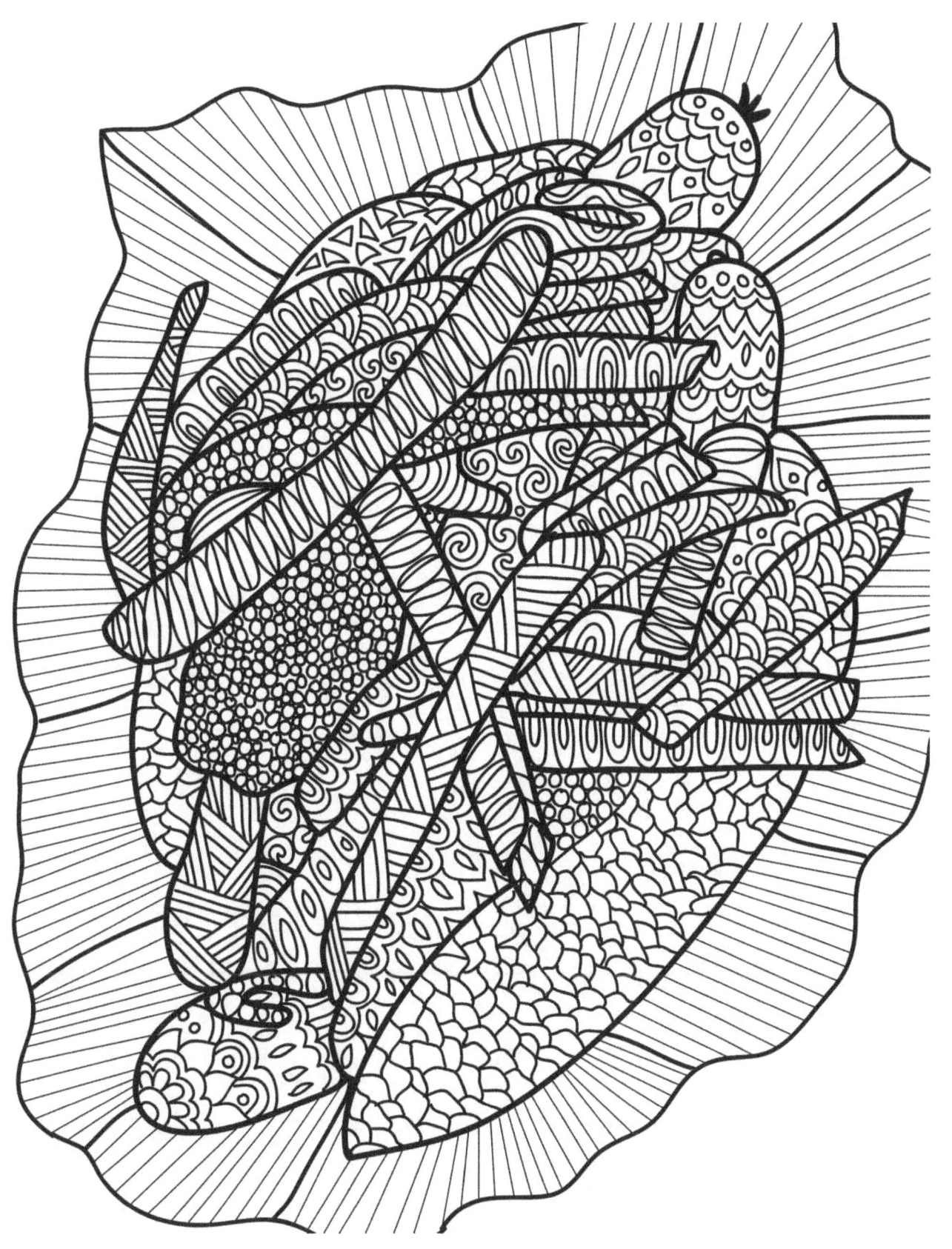

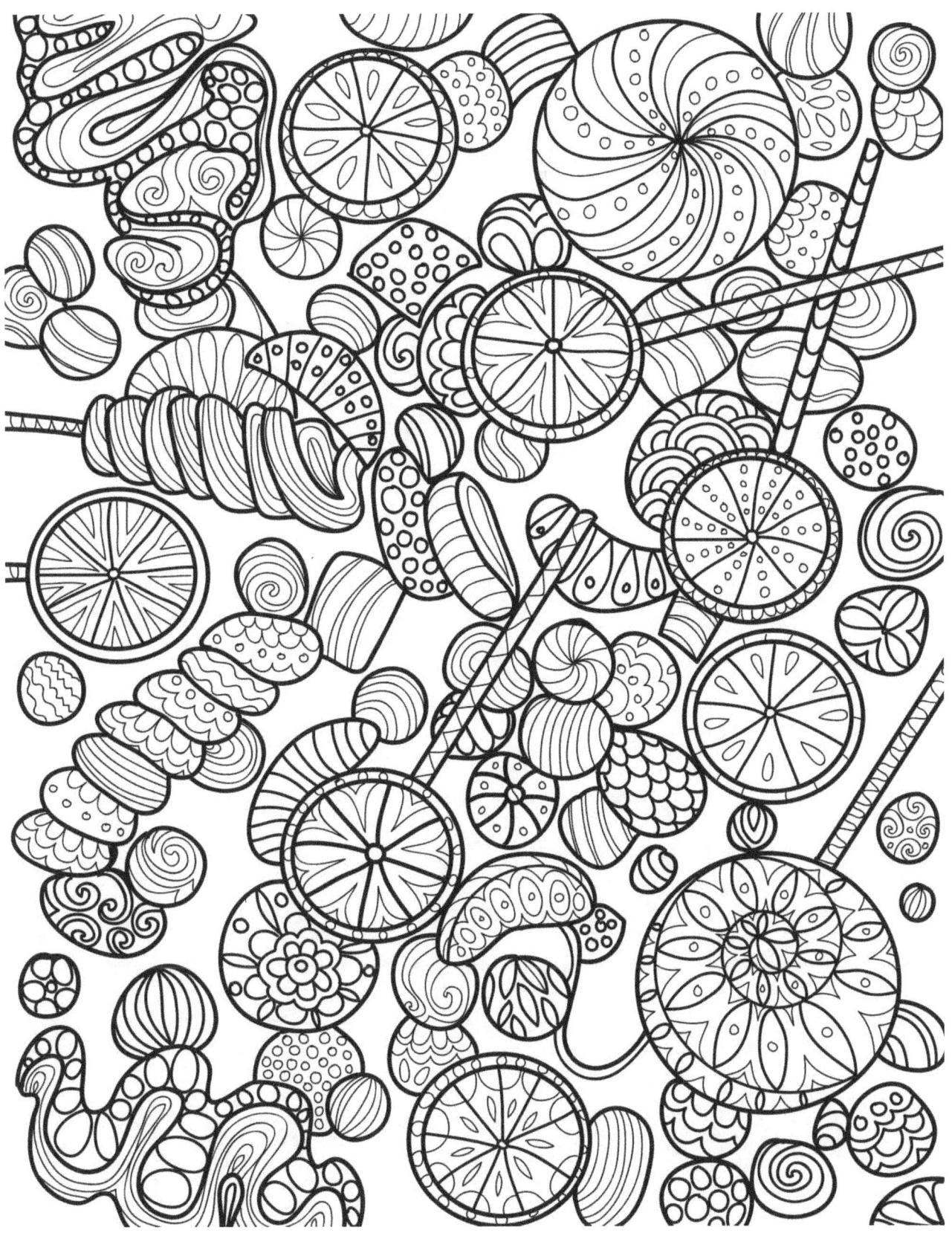

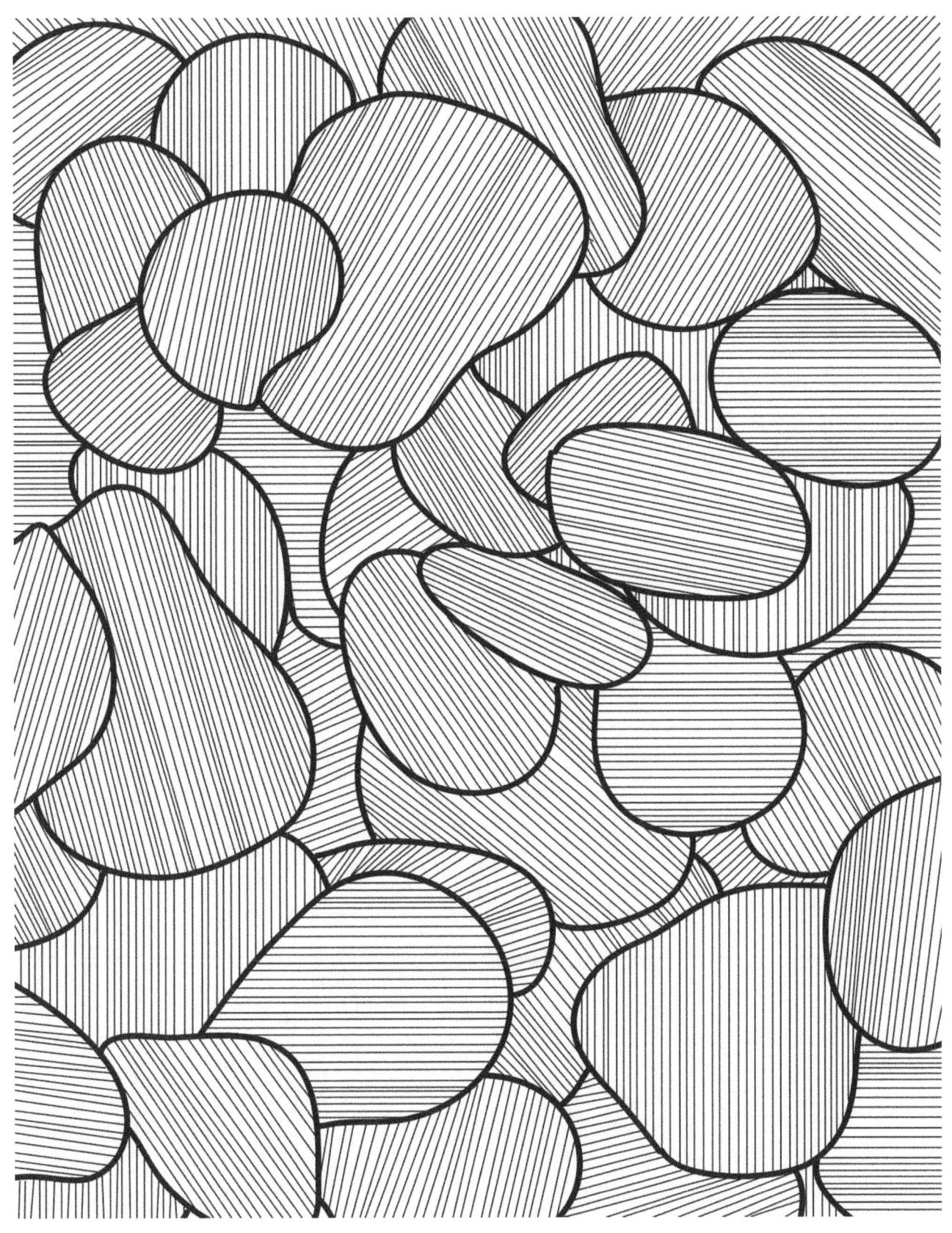

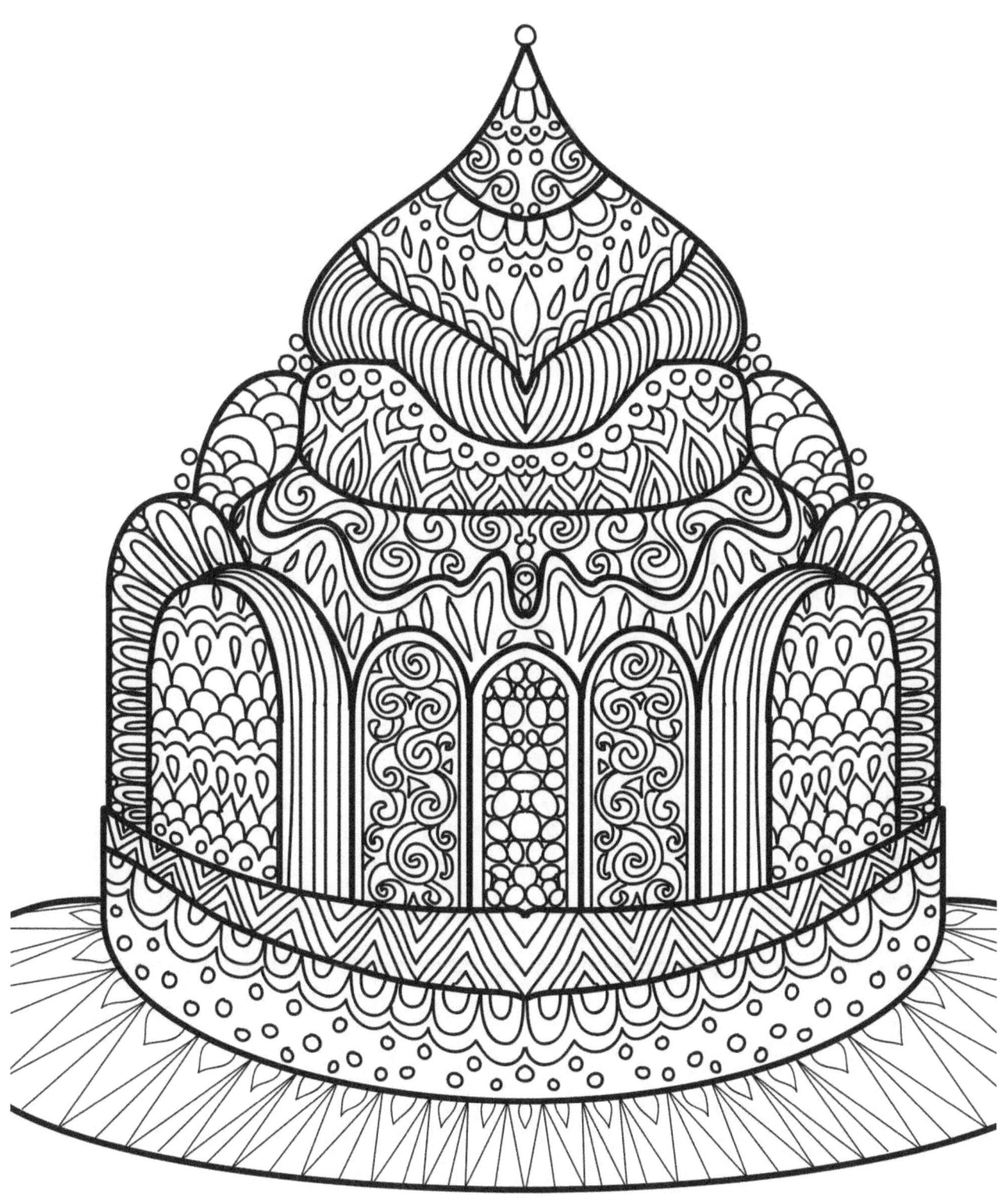

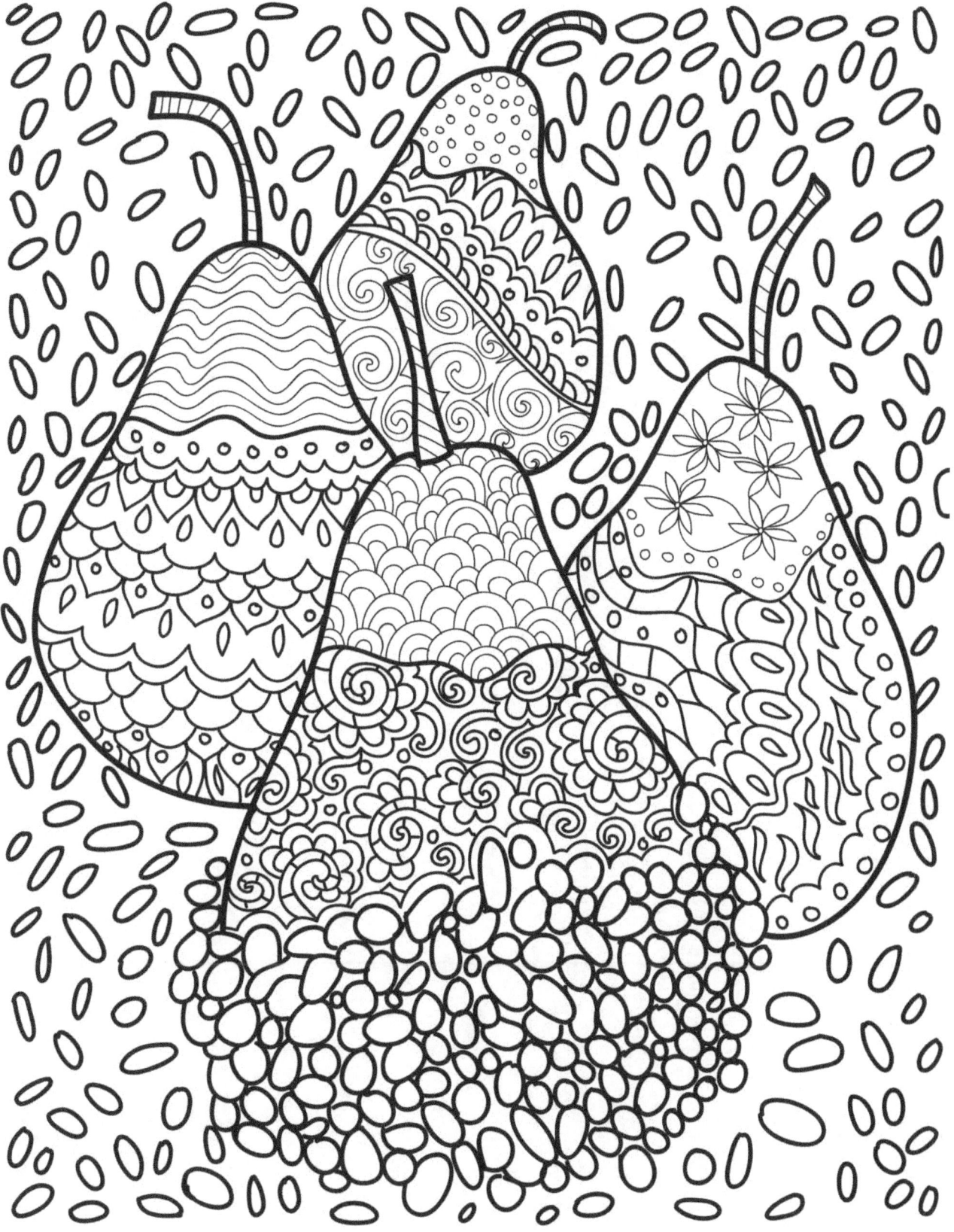

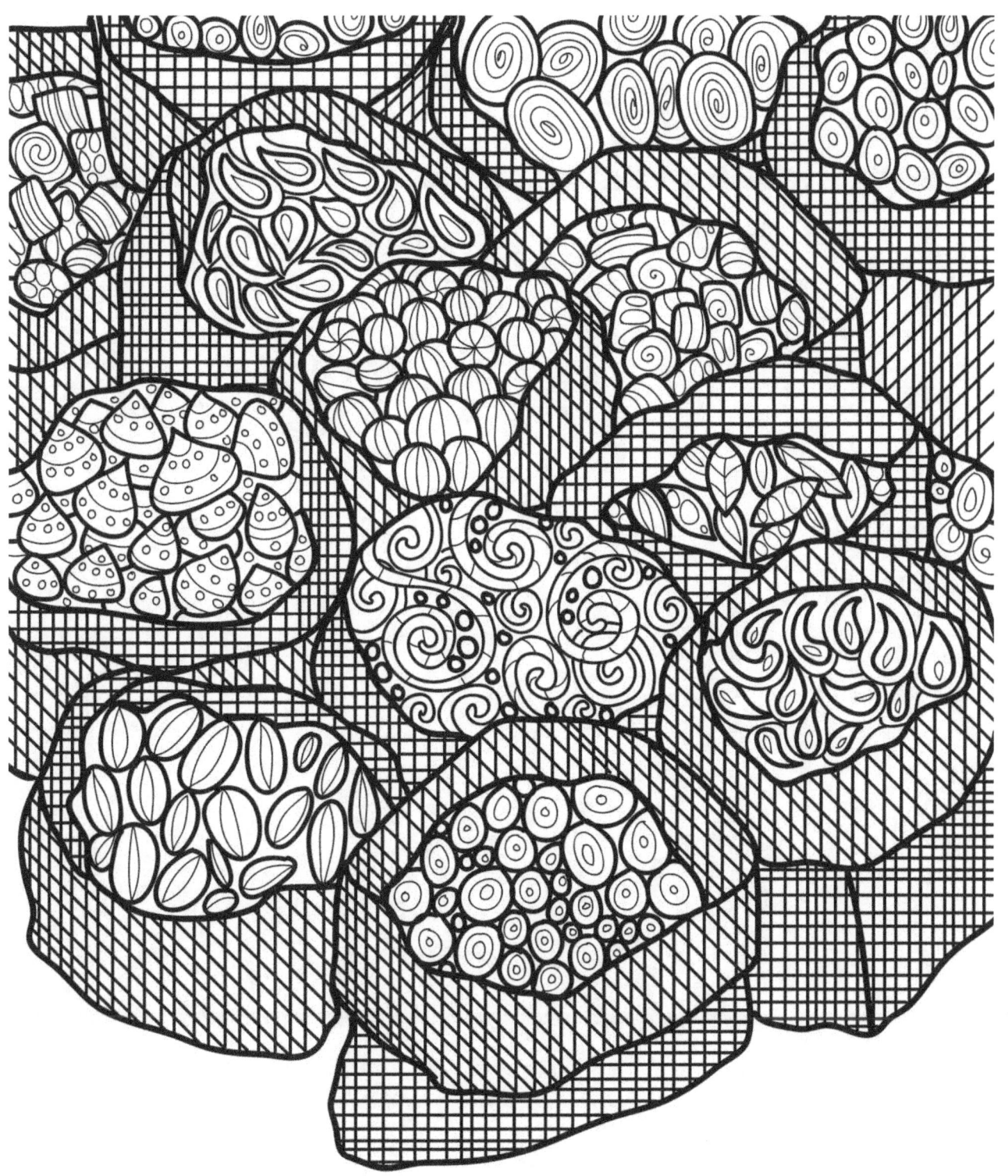

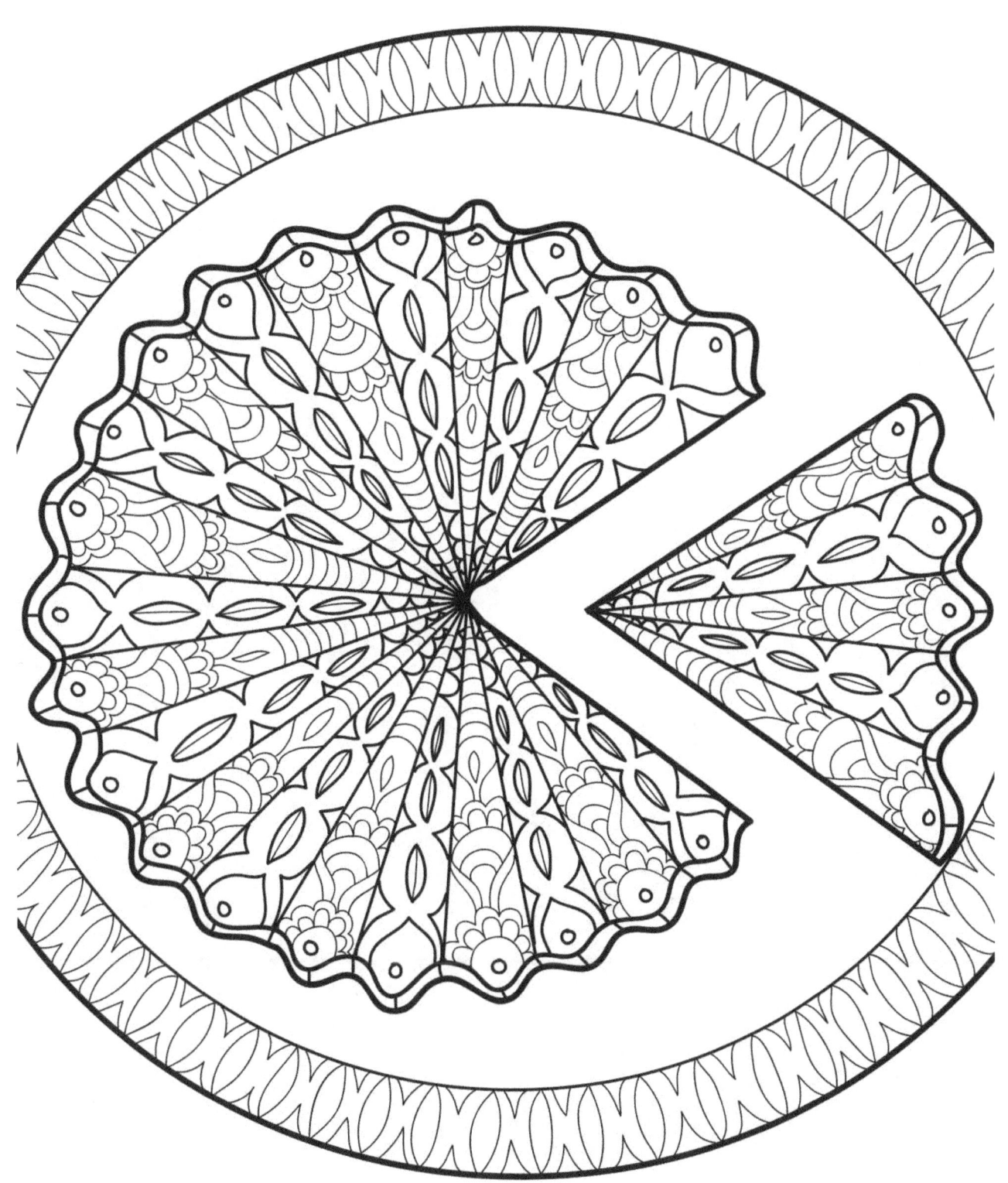

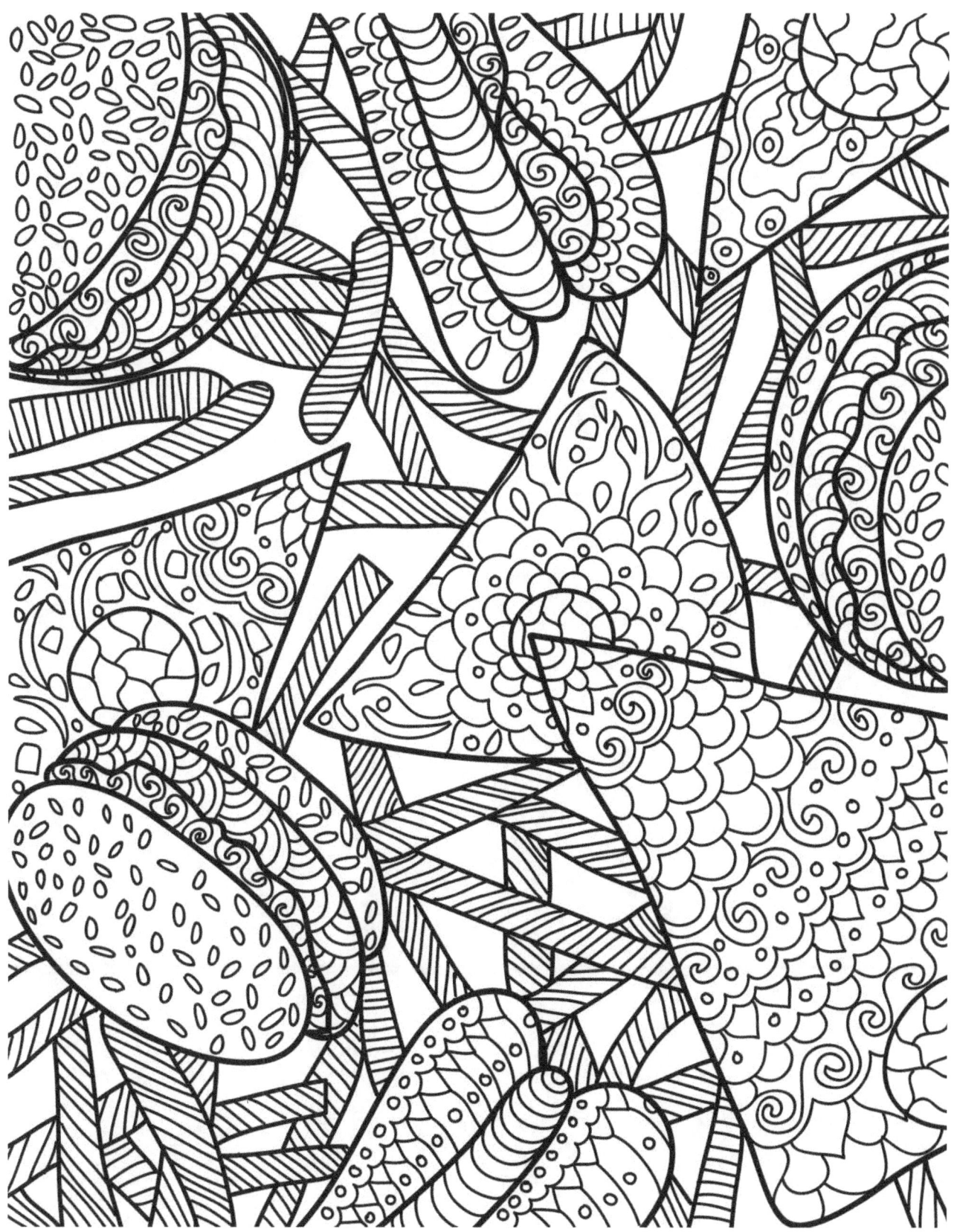

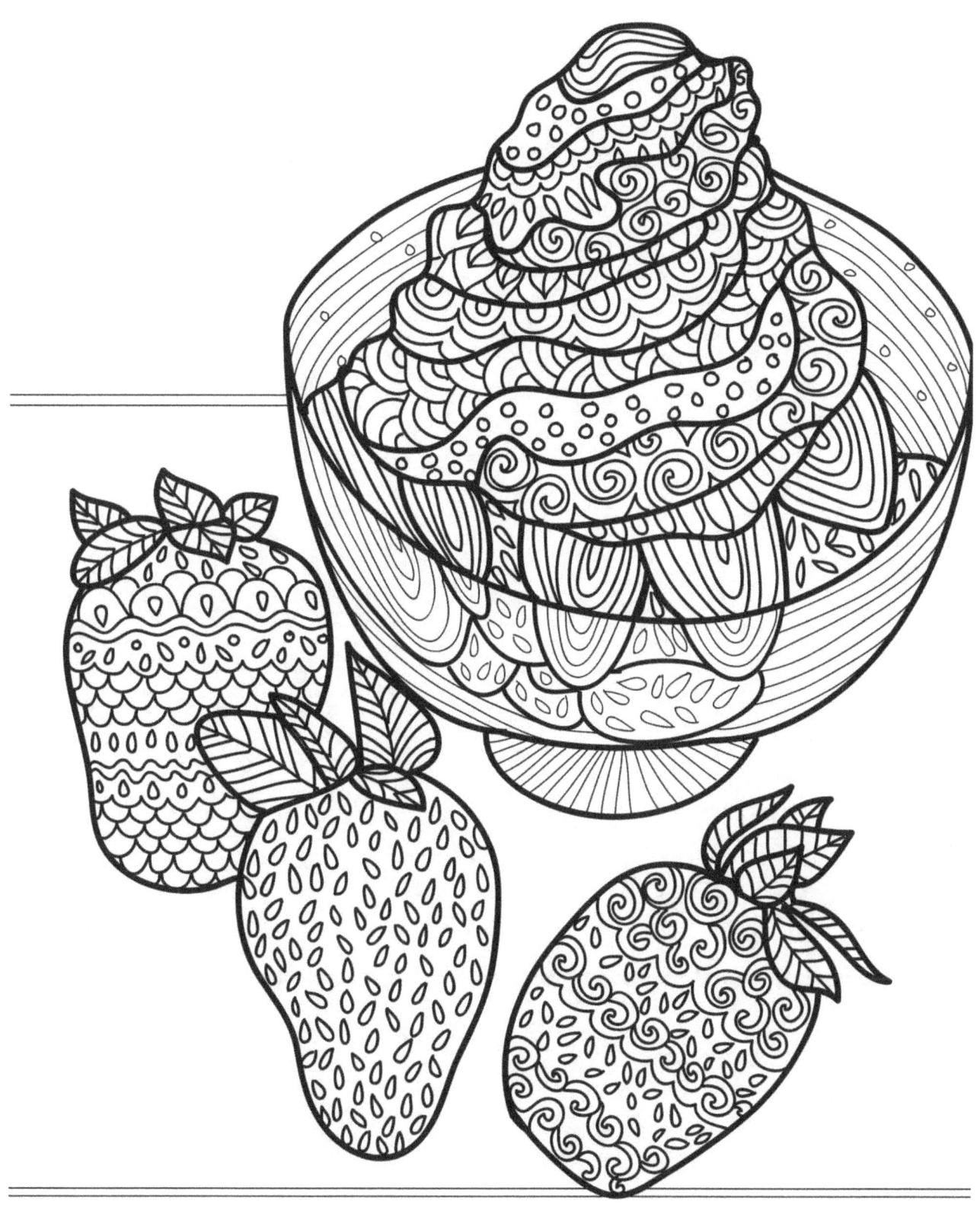

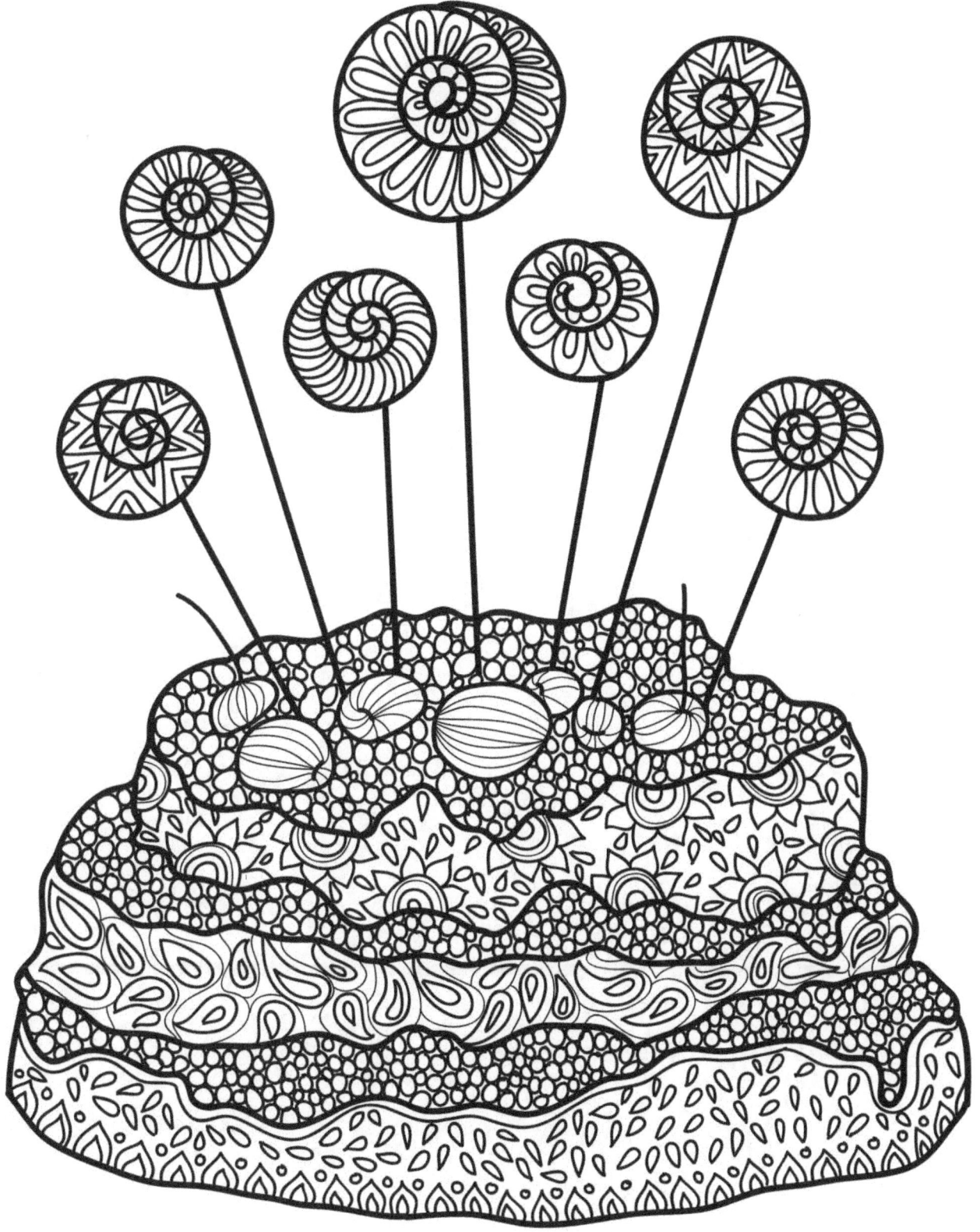

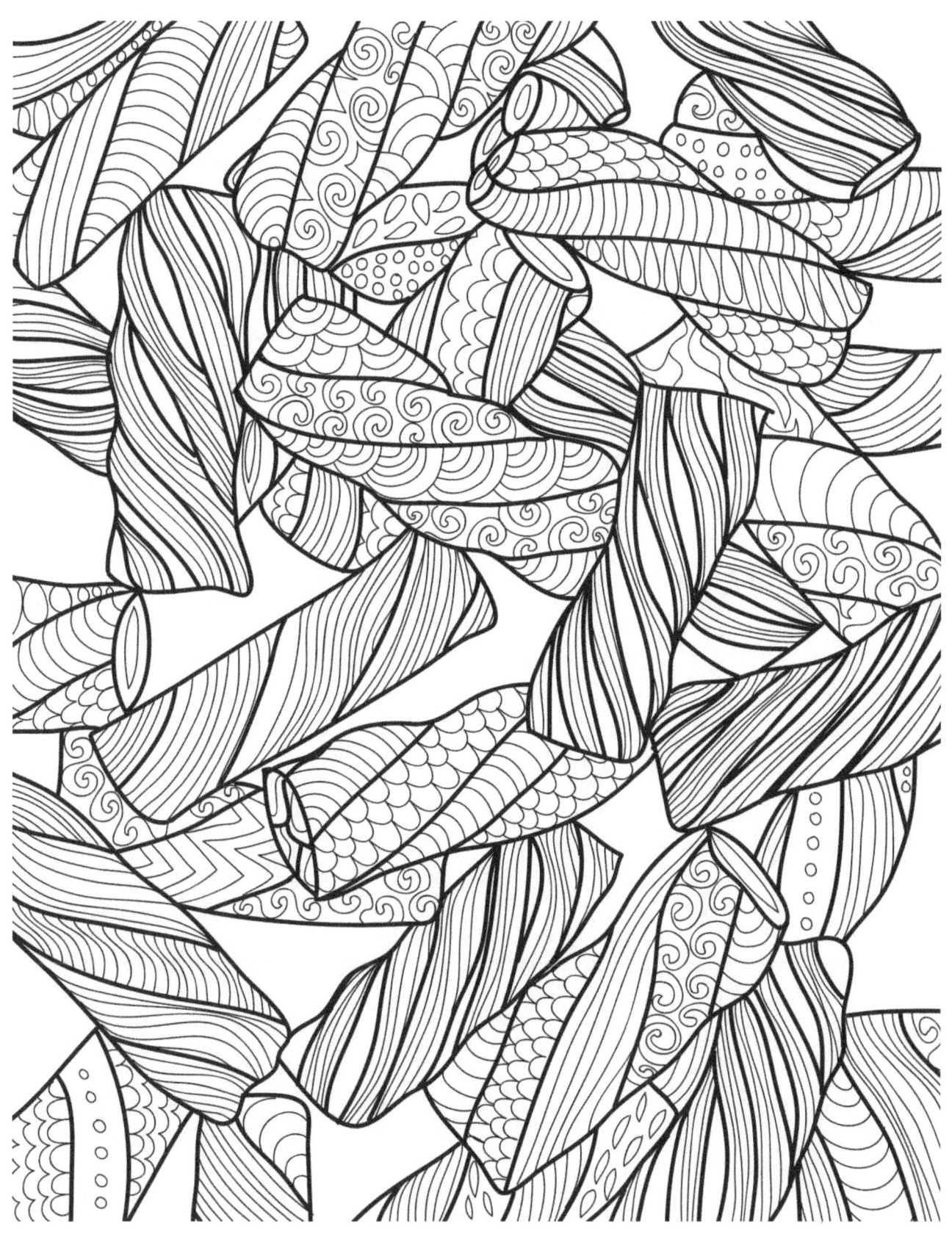

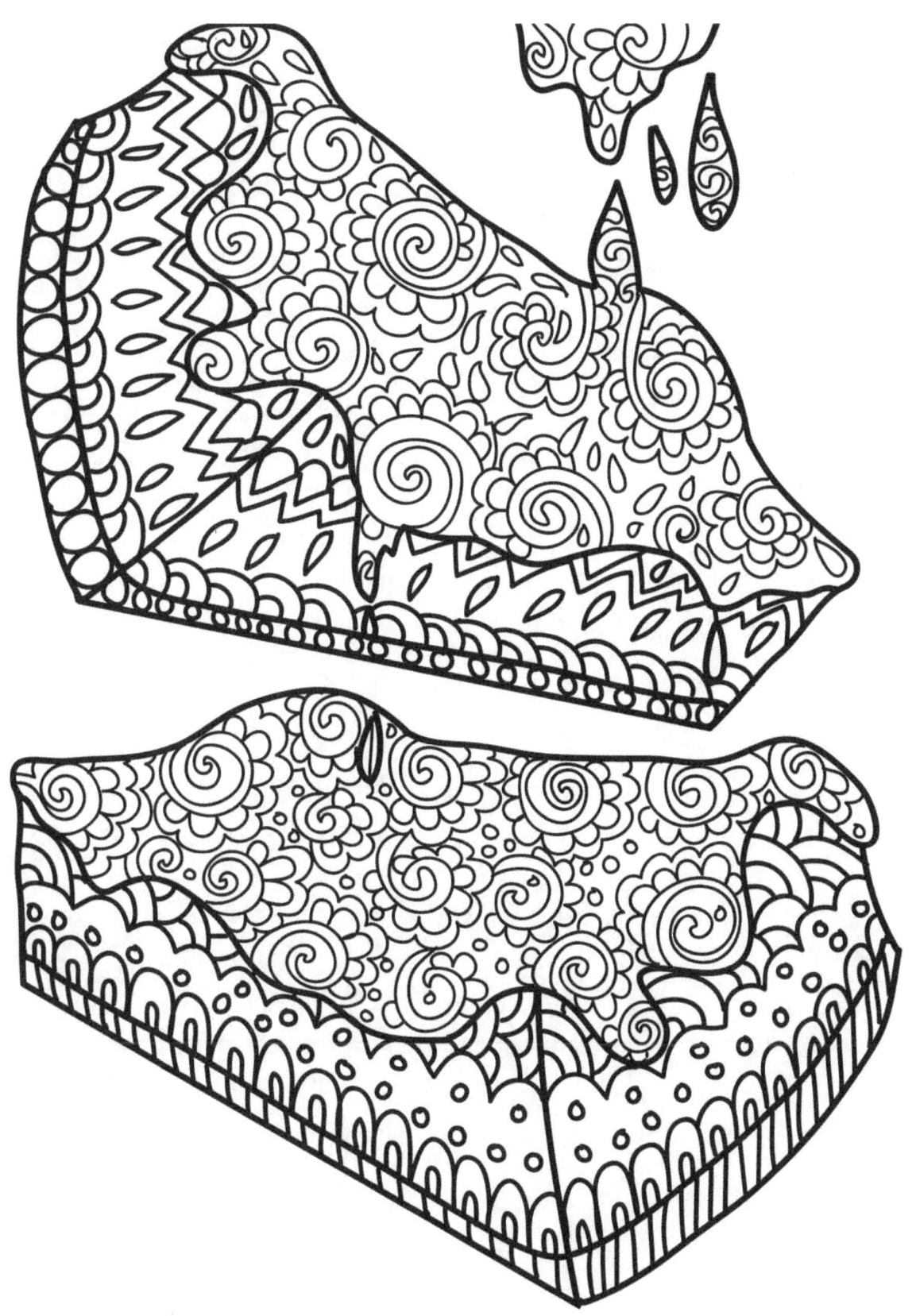

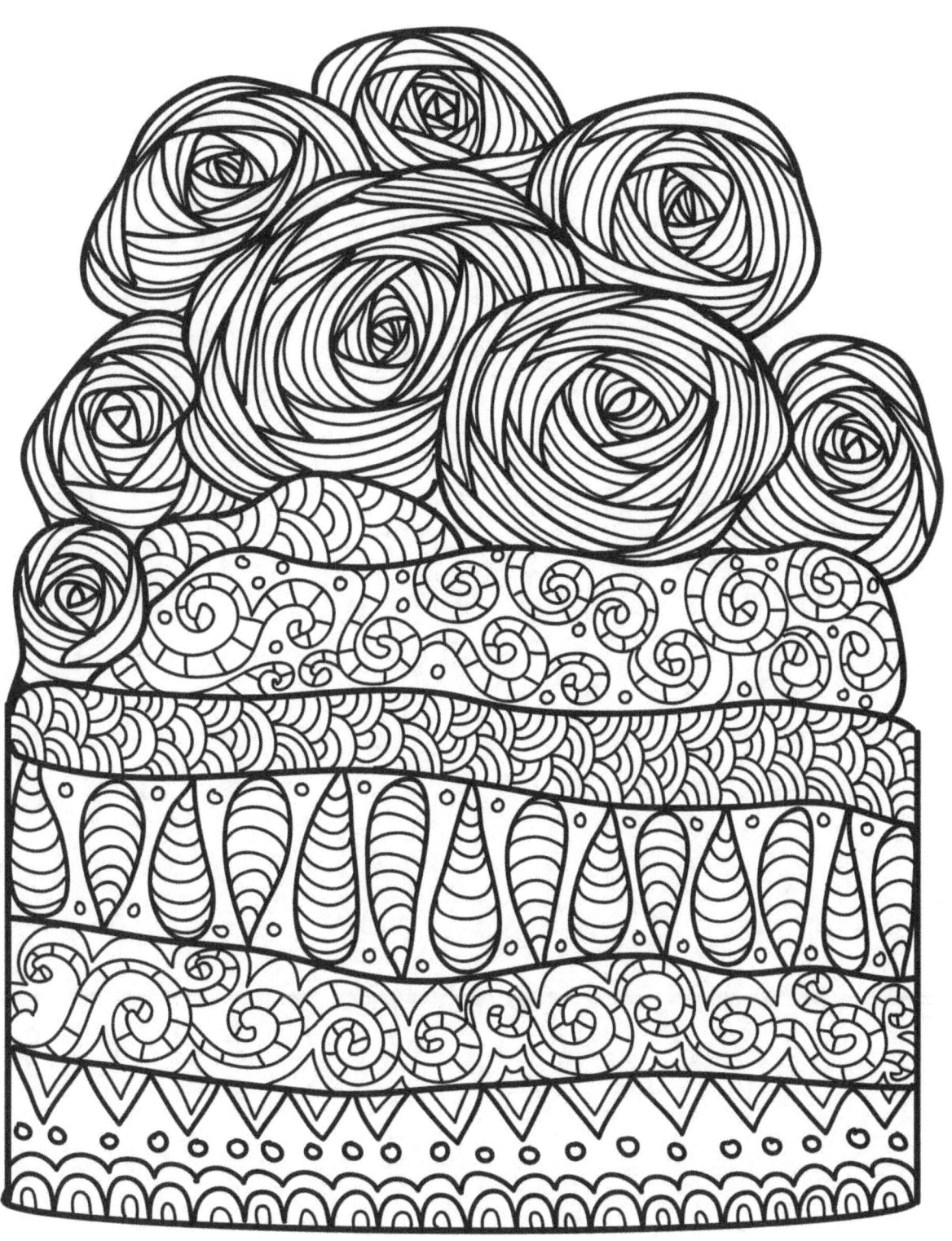

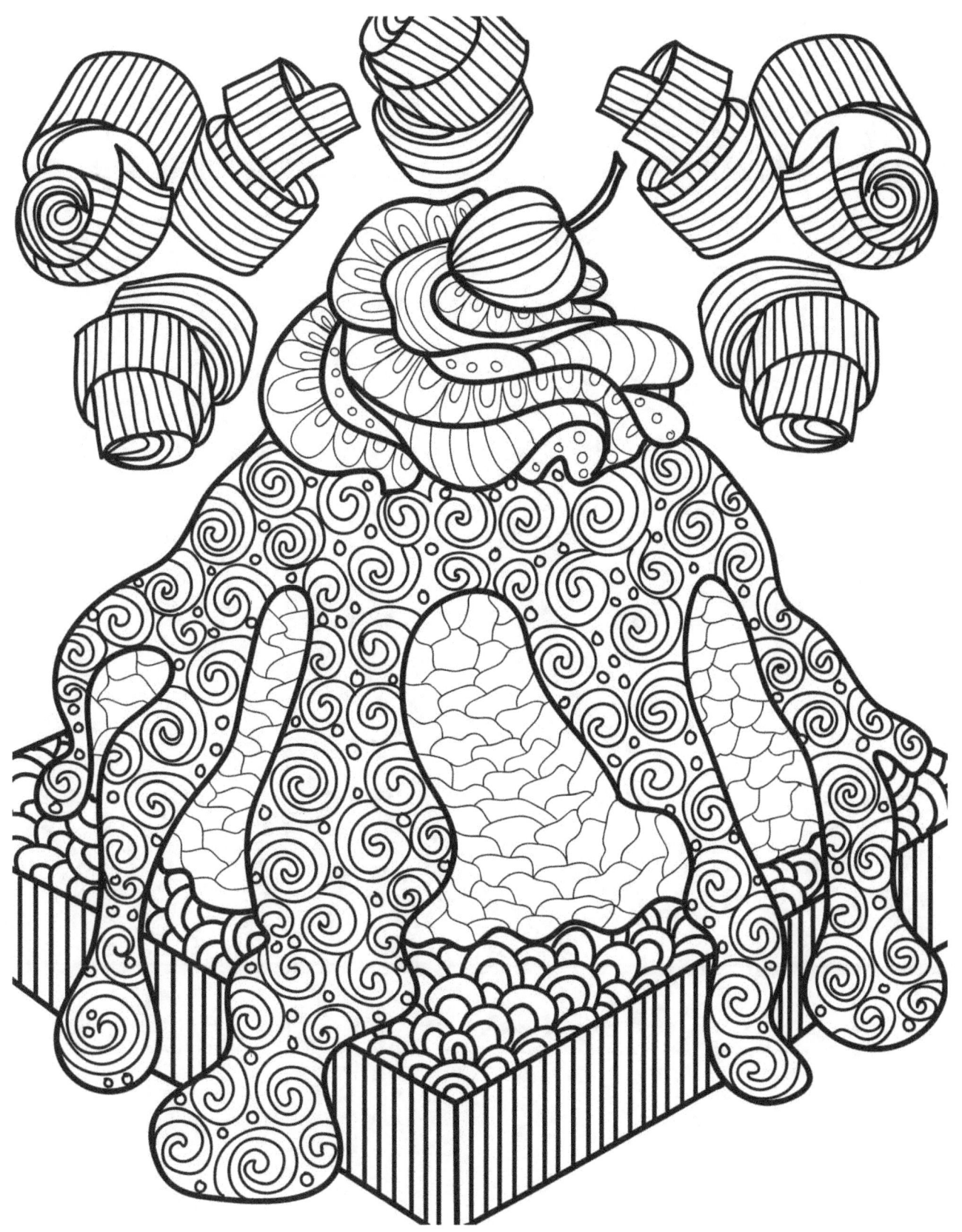

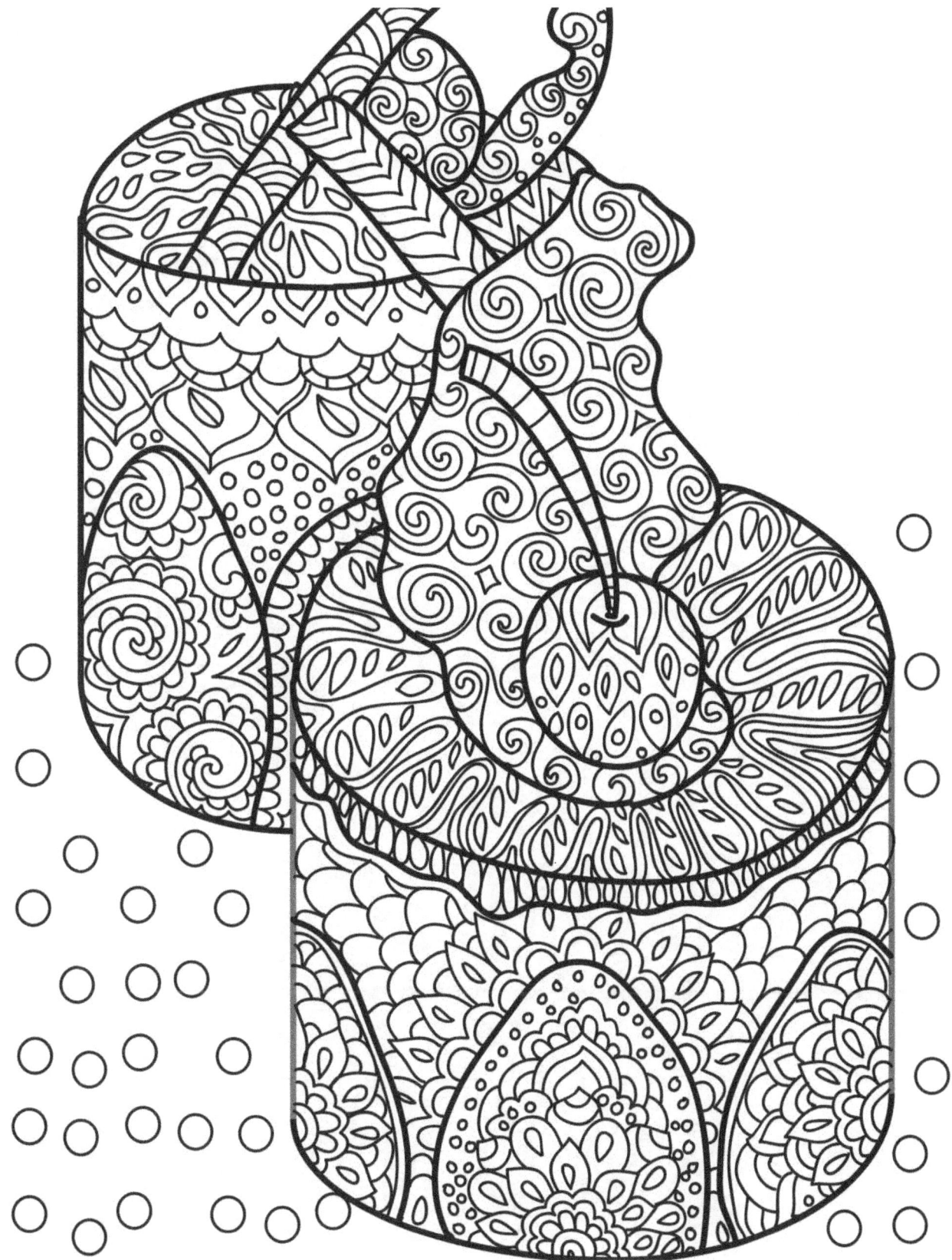

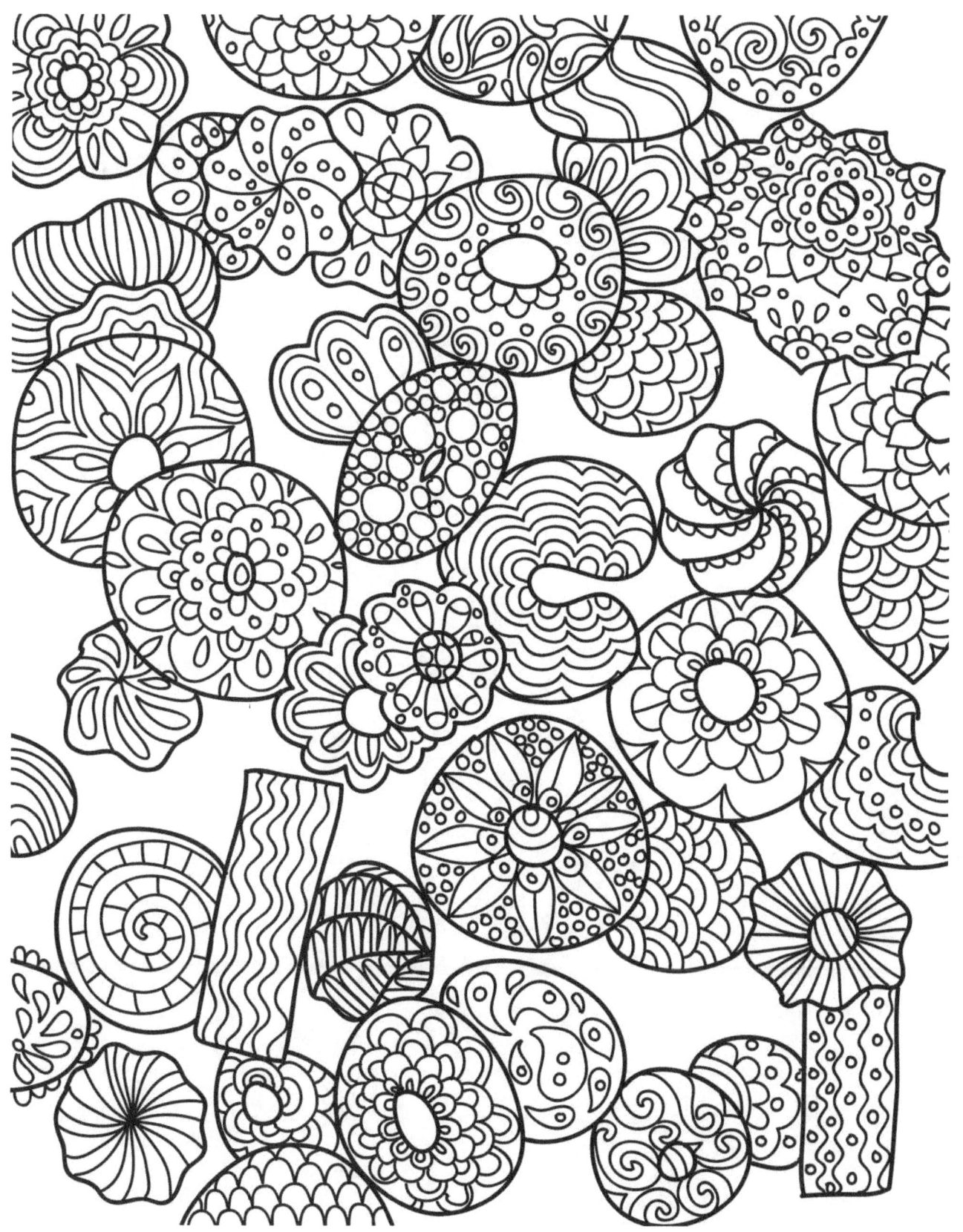

Hope you enjoyed all the custom designed images for your coloring pleasure!

Please keep an eye out for new coloring books or visit stressfreecoloring.org for new options from me and info regarding other newly released coloring books!

www.ingramcontent.com/pod-product-compliance
Lightning Source LLC
Chambersburg PA
CBHW080634190526
45169CB00009B/3390